AMERICAN BISON

Meryl Magby

PowerKiDS
press

New York

Published in 2012 by The Rosen Publishing Group, Inc.
29 East 21st Street, New York, NY 10010

First Edition

Editor: Amelie von Zumbusch
Book Design: Ashley Drago

Photo Credits: Cover Michael Wheatley/Getty Images; pp. 4, 14, 20–21, 22 Shutterstock.com; p. 5 © www.iStockphoto.com/David Mathies; p. 6 © www.iStockphoto.com/Aaron Pratt; pp. 7, 12–13 iStockphoto/Thinkstock; pp. 8–9 © www.iStockphoto.com/Bartosz Wardzinski; p. 10 © www.iStockphoto.com/Jonathan Eden; p. 11 © www.iStockphoto.com/Catharina van den Dikkenberg; p. 15 (right) © www.iStockphoto.com/Glenn Nagel; p. 15 (left) Gerald & Buff Corsi/Getty Images; p. 16 Susan Hilton/Getty Images; p. 17 © www.iStockphoto.com/Len Tillim; p. 18 George Catlin/Getty Images; p. 19 Eastcott Momatiuk/Getty Images.

Library of Congress Cataloging-in-Publication Data

Magby, Meryl.
 American bison / by Meryl Magby. — 1st ed.
   p. cm. — (American animals)
Includes index.
ISBN 978-1-4488-6179-8 (library binding) — ISBN 978-1-4488-6317-4 (pbk.) — ISBN 978-1-4488-6318-1 (6-pack)
1. Bison—Juvenile literature. I. Title.
QL737.U53M2236 2012
599.64'3—dc23

                          2011022733

Manufactured in the United States of America

CPSIA Compliance Information: Batch #WW12PK: For Further Information contact Rosen Publishing, New York, New York at 1-800-237-9932

Contents

Bison or Buffalo?

The American bison is a large **mammal** that lives in parts of the United States and Canada. In fact, male bison are the largest land mammals in North America. Scientists think that there were about 60 million wild bison roaming the **Great Plains** when European **explorers** came to North America. Today, there are only about half a million bison in North America.

Their size and strength make bison one of North America's most powerful animals.

These American bison are in Wyoming's Grand Teton National Park.

Bison are commonly called buffalo. This is because early European explorers thought that bison looked like African buffalo and Asian buffalo. Bison are related to these animals, but not closely. Both bison and buffalo are in the same animal family as cows, goats, and sheep.

Humps, Hooves, and Horns

As you can see, bison have shaggier fur on the front of their bodies.

Bison are known for having large heads, small hips, and humps on their backs. Like cows and sheep, bison have **cloven** hooves. These are hooves with two toes.

Bison have thick, woolly coats in the winter that they shed as it becomes warmer. Their coats may be dark brown

or light brown depending on where they live. Both male and female bison have **hollow**, curved horns. Male bison weigh about 2,000 pounds (907 kg). They are about 6 feet (2 m) tall at their shoulders. Female bison are much smaller. They weigh around 1,100 pounds (500 kg) and stand about 5 feet (1.5 m) tall.

Bison do not have very good eyesight. They can smell and hear very well, though.

Bison in North America

At one time, American bison roamed grasslands and forests all over North America. Scientists think that bison crossed over a land bridge from Asia to North America thousands of years ago. Early European explorers and settlers found millions of bison **grazing** the plains and prairies between the Mississippi River and the Rocky Mountains.

These bison are in Yellowstone National Park. This park is in Idaho, Montana, and Wyoming.

Today, wild bison are found on **public** lands in Nebraska, Montana, Wyoming, North Dakota, South Dakota, Oklahoma, Iowa, Utah, Arizona, Minnesota, Alaska, Kansas, Wisconsin, Idaho, and Kentucky. Many bison also live in private herds. Most of these bison are raised for their meat.

Grazing Herds

An adult bison eats about 35 pounds (16 kg) of food each day.

Bison are **herbivores**. This means they eat only plants. Bison move around throughout the day, grazing as they go. Though they eat mostly grasses, bison also graze on other kinds of plants, such as forbs and sedges. In the winter, bison do not stop grazing even when snow

After a bison's stomach breaks down its food for the first time, the bison brings the food back into its mouth. It chews the food as cud before swallowing it for a second time.

covers the plains. They swing their wide heads from side to side to sweep away the snow.

Bison graze in herds. Herds travel about 5 miles per hour (8 km/h) while grazing. A herd of grazing bison generally travels about 10 to 15 miles (16–24 km) a day.

Bison Facts

1. Although they are large, bison move quickly. They can run at speeds of up to 30 miles per hour (48 km/h). They can turn around faster than a horse.

2. Bison often roll on their backs to cover themselves in dust or mud. This is called wallowing. The holes in the ground that bison make when they wallow are called wallows, too.

3. Birds, such as magpies, sometimes ride on the backs of bison. This is because they eat insects that live in the bison's coats.

4. Ancient bison were much bigger than the bison that live today. One kind of ancient bison, *Bison latifrons*, had horns that were 9 feet (3 m) long from tip to tip.

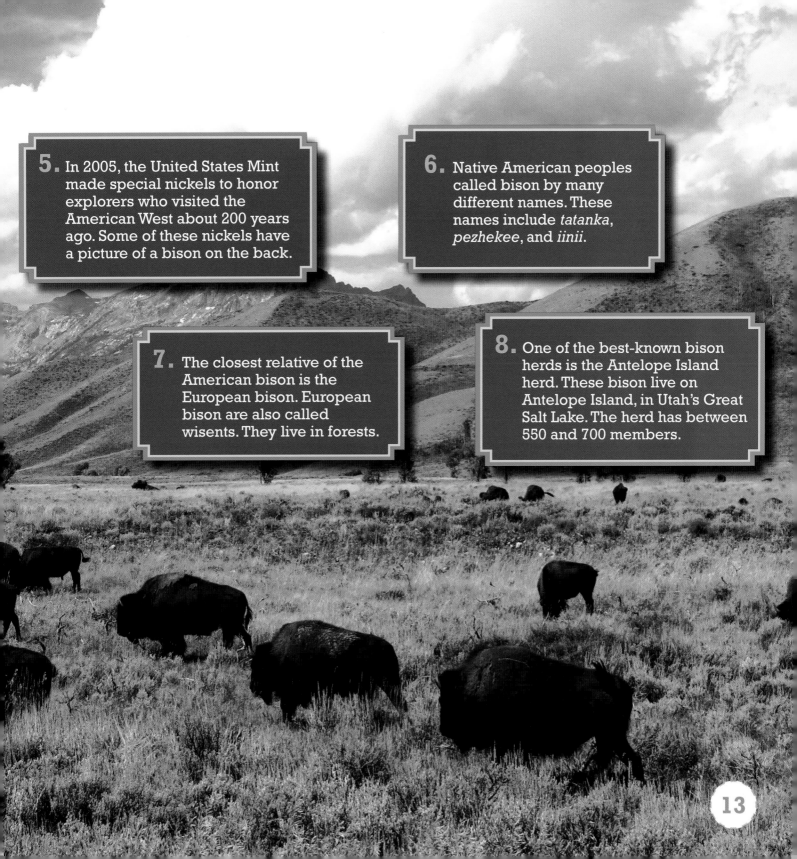

5. In 2005, the United States Mint made special nickels to honor explorers who visited the American West about 200 years ago. Some of these nickels have a picture of a bison on the back.

6. Native American peoples called bison by many different names. These names include *tatanka*, *pezhekee*, and *iinii*.

7. The closest relative of the American bison is the European bison. European bison are also called wisents. They live in forests.

8. One of the best-known bison herds is the Antelope Island herd. These bison live on Antelope Island, in Utah's Great Salt Lake. The herd has between 550 and 700 members.

Groups of Bison

Groups of cows and young bison tend to be led by one of the older cows. The other bison follow her around as she finds places to graze and drink.

Large groups of bison that live on the same **range** are called herds. Herds often include smaller groups of bison that live closely together. Female bison, or cows, often live together in groups of between 20 and 60 bison with their babies and young male bison. Male bison are called bulls. Bulls that are old enough to **mate** tend to live alone or in small groups of other **mature** bulls.

When two animals fight by pushing against each other with their heads, it is known as butting heads. These bulls are butting heads.

During the mating season, bison bulls let out loud cries called bellows.

Each July, mating season starts. This is also called the rut. During this time, mature bulls fight with each other over which cows they will mate with. The bulls crash their heads together and hook their horns.

15

Cows and Calves

Bison calves do not start to grow their shoulder humps or horns until they are about two months old.

Baby bison are called calves. Cows most often give birth to one calf a year. Most calves are born in April and May. Bison calves are a reddish-orange color when they are born. Their coats start to turn brown when they are about three months old.

Calves start to walk when they are just 3 hours old. At first, they drink their mothers' milk. Soon, they start eating grass as well.

This calf is a newborn. Its mother is licking it clean. When they give birth, cows often go off on their own for a few days.

Calves stay with their mothers for about a year. Bison become old enough to mate when they are about two years old. Most bison live for about 12 to 15 years, though some live longer.

Bison and Native Americans

Bison were a very important part of life for Native American peoples on the Great Plains. For thousands of years before Europeans came to North America, Plains Indians lived among large herds of bison. These peoples hunted bison for their meat. They also used bison fur, skin, and

American Indians used several methods to hunt bison. This picture shows some Native American hunters creeping up on a herd of bison while wearing wolf skins.

Some of the Native American peoples who depended on bison were the Kiowas, Cheyennes, Assiniboines, Lakotas, and Comanches.

bones to build homes and to make clothing and tools.

When Europeans reached North America and began moving west, they hunted bison in huge numbers. The number of wild bison got smaller and smaller. By the 1800s, so many people were hunting bison that they were in danger of dying out.

Protecting Bison

In the 1800s, hunters and fur traders killed hundreds of thousands of wild bison for their meat and fur. Wild bison were also killed to make room for **livestock** and railroads. By 1900, there were fewer than 300 wild bison left in the United States and Canada. Many people became worried that bison would die out totally if laws were not made to **protect** them.

> Today, Yellowstone National Park is home to several thousand American bison.

In 1894, Congress made it illegal to hunt bison in Yellowstone National Park. Anyone who killed a bison there had to pay $1,000 or be thrown in jail. Since then, the size of protected herds on public lands has slowly grown.

Bison Today

Thanks to laws protecting bison, they are no longer in danger of dying out. There are now more than 500,000 bison living in North America. Some of these bison live in private herds, while others are wild.

Today, many wild bison live in national parks or wildlife **refuges**, such as Theodore Roosevelt National Park in North Dakota, Fort Niobrara National Wildlife Refuge in Nebraska, and Wichita Mountains National Wildlife Refuge in Oklahoma. If you want to see wild bison, you could visit one of these places!

Happily, bison are making a comeback. These huge animals should be around for years to come.

Glossary

cloven (KLOH-ven) Having two toes.

explorers (ek-SPLOR-erz) People who travel and look for new land.

grazing (GRAY-zing) Feeding on grass.

Great Plains (GRAYT PLAYNZ) Flat, grassy land in the middle of North America.

herbivores (ER-buh-vorz) Animals that eat only plants.

hollow (HOL-oh) Having a hole through the center.

livestock (LYV-stok) Animals raised by people.

mammal (MA-mul) A warm-blooded animal that has a backbone and hair, breathes air, and feeds milk to its young.

mate (MAYT) To come together to make babies.

mature (muh-TOOR) Fully grown.

protect (pruh-TEKT) To keep safe.

public (PUH-blik) Owned by the government.

range (RAYNJ) The distance something can travel.

refuges (REH-fyoo-jez) Places where things are kept safe.

Index

B
back(s), 6, 12–13
buffalo, 5
bulls, 14–15

C
Canada, 4, 20
cows, 5–6, 14–16

G
goats, 5
Great Plains, 4, 18

H
heads, 6, 11, 15
herbivores, 10
hips, 6
horns, 7, 12, 15

L
lands, 8, 20
livestock, 20

M
mammal(s), 4

N
North America, 4, 8, 18–19, 22

P
people(s), 13, 18–20

S
scientists, 4, 8
settlers, 8
sheep, 5–6

Web Sites

Due to the changing nature of Internet links, PowerKids Press has developed an online list of Web sites related to the subject of this book. This site is updated regularly. Please use this link to access the list:
www.powerkidslinks.com/aman/bison/